Moments With Britan
A Therapy Dog

By Barbara J. Peters

Art By Joan Coleman

Alpharetta, Georgia

Copyright © 2025 by Barbara J. Peters

All rights reserved. No part of this publication may be reproduced or distributed in any form or by any means, or stored in a database or retrieval system, without the prior written consent of Barbara Peters, at barbarajpeters.com, including, but not limited to, network storage or transmission, or broadcast for distance learning. Characters, businesses, places, events, and incidents are used in a fictitious manner. Any resemblance to actual people, living or dead, places, or actual events is purely coincidental.

ISBN: 978-1-6653-1086-4 - Paperback
ISBN: 978-1-6653-1087-1- Hardcover

Library of Congress Control Number: 2025913046

Printed in the United States of America

∞ This paper meets the requirements of ANSI/NISO Z39.48-1992 (Permanence of Paper)

Illustrations by Joan Coleman
Photo of Barbara and Britan by Rich Taylor, www.richtaylorphotography.com

061925

Dedication

I dedicate this book to all therapy dogs, their handlers and the organizations that certify them with a special thank you to Alliance of Therapy Dogs. It is because of them that people who are sick, lonely and in stressful situations can receive the love and compassion that these special animals provide.

My name is Britan, and I am a dog. Not just any dog, though. I am a therapy dog. Do you know what that is?

To be a therapy dog, I had to go to school and pass a test.

At school, I learned to walk through crowded places, go in and out of elevators, ignore distractions, and most importantly—say no to any treats from people.

Wow, this is the hardest one for me. I love treats!

Let me tell you a little about myself. I am a Cavalier King Charles spaniel, and I *love* people. My personality is calm and friendly. My tail wags a lot.

I am nine years old and have spent many years bringing smiles and joy to people as a therapy dog. But I couldn't do it alone!

My Mom and I are a team. She brings me everywhere and makes sure we pay attention to all the rules to do our job.

Now, huddle up! I've been waiting a long time to tell everyone about my adventures, and you look like you're ready to hear them! Are you?

Today, I am in a classroom with special needs children. These children are different because they needed a little extra time and help to learn.

Some are unsure of me and a little afraid.
I understand this because I was once afraid too.

My job here is to show how dogs can make
them feel safe and calm, and make learning fun.

The teacher is happy to have me there. The kids warm up to me, some even pet me, while others ask questions. They sit in a circle with me in the middle so everyone can see me. I love that!

Here I am at the Assisted Living Facility. This is where grandpas and grandmas live when they can't live alone anymore.

They get help with things like getting dressed, making food, and cleaning their rooms. They also make new friends here.

Mom has told me that many of them are sad because they can't bring their pets, but when they see me, their faces light up with happy smiles. They get good care here and I am happy to cheer them up.

Not everyone wants to pet me or talk to me, but I don't mind. I understand this, and do not try to encourage them to do so.

I am now at a college. This is a school where students go after high school to learn how to get a grown-up job. I am here with other therapy dogs to help the students feel calm when taking their final exams. Taking tests can be stressful, I know.

Lots of students live at the college and cannot see their dogs all the time. They talk about how they miss them. They are happy to see me and the other therapy dogs.

Here I am, at the busy airport, full of people. I wear a vest that says PET ME and lots of people do just that.

Some people are waiting to take a trip, and some have just come back.
Some are just afraid to fly on a plane.

When they walk by and see me, they stop to pet me.

For a few minutes, they forget about their fear of flying, or of having to wait so long. I like helping people.

At the library, I get to see lots of kids!

Some are excited to read to me, while others aren't sure. They may even be a bit scared.

I am here to make them feel comfortable while reading. Reading to a dog can do just that!

I am a good listener too, and I even like the pictures they show me!

They often pet me while they read, and it makes me happy to help them enjoy their books and see them smile!

When I go to the hospital, I see people who are sick.

Some are in bed, others in wheelchairs.

I must be especially quiet here, and my mom helps me to stay out of the way of medical equipment.

Sometimes, she must pick me up and bring me closer to the patient so they can pet me.

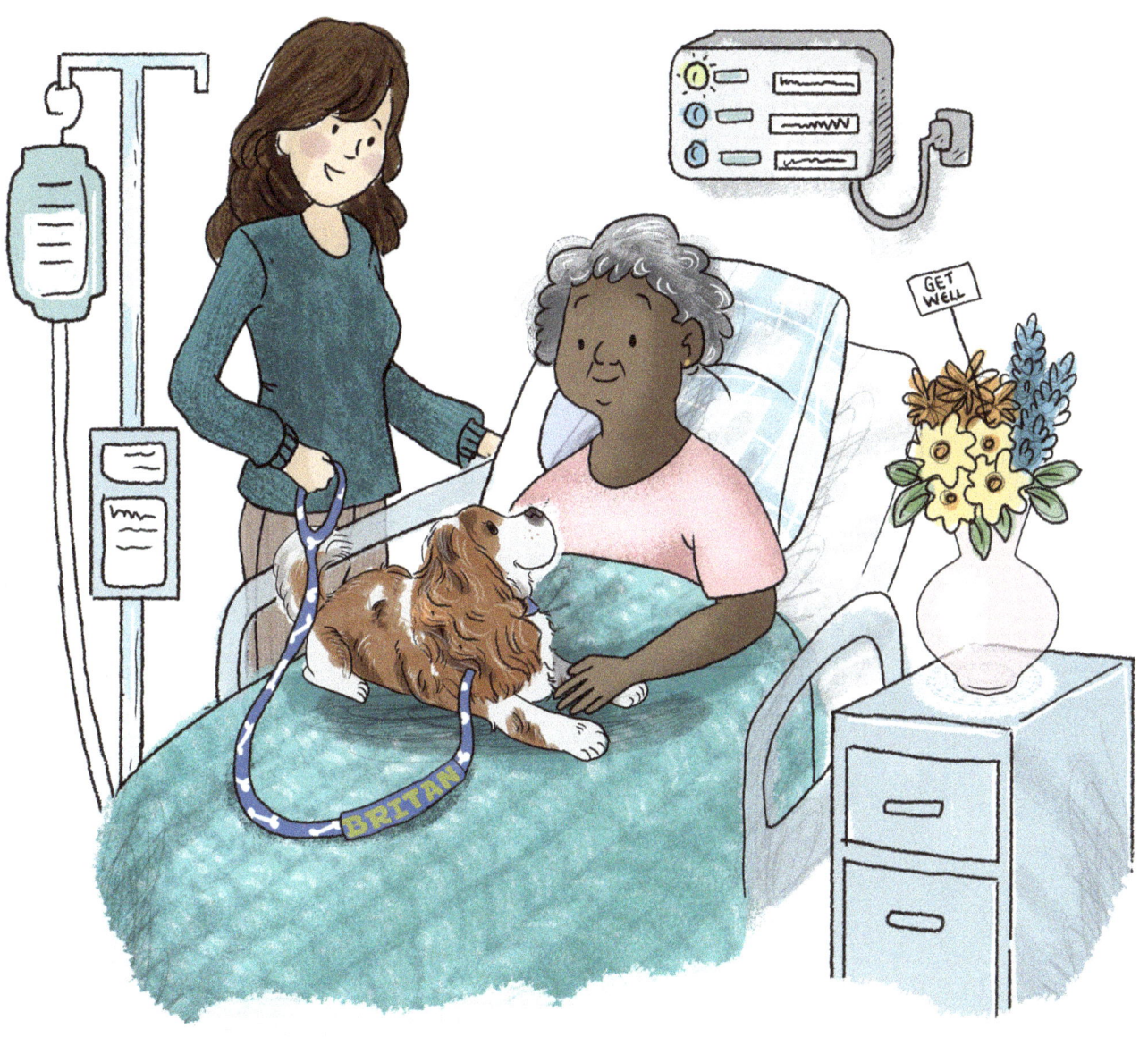

The nurses are happy when I come to see their patients. I help them feel better and this makes me happy too.

After a long day of spreading smiles and joy, there is no better way to unwind than by spending time with my mother, father, and two Cavalier sisters.

Do you wonder how you might bring smiles and joy to someone's heart? I bet you can think of some ways to do just that. And guess what, it will bring you happiness too!

About The Author

Working with my therapy dog, Britan, a Cavalier King Charles spaniel, has been a high point in my life and immensely rewarding. As a team, Britan and I have spent many hours in assisted living facilities, the Charlotte Douglas airport, libraries, classrooms, hospitals, adolescent treatment centers, and universities, bringing people smiles and joy. The people love his visits and are grateful for the service Britan and other therapy dogs deliver.

Britan's fondness for children at the library has been special. *Moments with Britan* was written to show children the benefits therapy dogs provide. Britan—in his own voice—talks about his experiences and the many places he has brought joy to others.

About The Illustrator

Joan Coleman is a professional artist and book illustrator. She and her husband, Andrew, own and operate Ink Wonderland, an illustration and design company that provides graphic design, illustration, and apparel design services for clients all across the USA.

www.ingramcontent.com/pod-product-compliance
Lightning Source LLC
Chambersburg PA
CBHW042355070526
44585CB00028B/2943